Read in

AF572015

a visit from MISS MARVIN

A heartwarming story of friendship and hope

To ALEXA,
Happy Reading

Donna Jean Paff

DONNA JEAN PAFF

Illustrated by Bella Viva

Aperture Press

Copyright © 2016 by Donna Jean Paff.

All rights reserved. Published by Aperture Press. Name and associated logos are trademarks and/or registered trademarks of Aperture Press, LLC.

No part of this publication may be reproduced, stored in a retrieval system, or transmitted in any form or by any means, electronic, mechanical, photocopying, recording, or otherwise, without written permission of the publisher. For information, write to Aperture Press LLC, P.O. Box 6485, Reading, PA 19610 or visit www.AperturePress.net.

ISBN: 978-0-9973020-1-1
Library of Congress Control Number: 2016943299

This is a work of fiction based on true events. Names, characters, places, and incidents are either the product of the author's imagination or are used fictitiously, and any resemblance to actual persons, living or dead, business establishments, events, or locales is entirely coincidental.

First edition, June 2016.

Book designed by Stephen Wagner.

This book is dedicated to Mr. Philip Smythe, whose light shone brightly on everyone equally. He made others feel special and was known for his kindness and grace. It was through this loving light that Miss Marvin developed her own unique glow and gave us a wonderful story.

This book became a reality through the encouragement of my dear friend, Ruth Miller, who opened the door for me to stretch my comfort zone and reach my goal of giving anyone reading this story their own personal visit from Miss Marvin.

PREFACE

The Story Of Miss Marvin: How It All Began

—

Creative writing is one of my favorite outlets and has given me hours of pleasure over the years, however writing a book that would become a published work had not been my intention. The book you are holding is a product of a fortunate stroke of serendipity (*occurring through happy coincidence*). Through an unexpected encounter with a fascinating cat named Miss Marvin, I was given an opportunity to affect the lives of others in a beneficial way by writing her story.

It all began during my job at an assisted living facility where I heard stories about a new resident's cat. Even the most difficult-to-please elders agreed that this cat named Miss Marvin had "magical powers" that could ease their discomfort much like my therapy did. Intrigued and amused, I grew eager to meet my "competition" in person.

When I arrived at his door Mr. Smythe (pronounced *Smith*) quickly invited me in for a chat and immediately introduced me to his cat,

Miss Marvin, who was standing by his side. As I knelt down to pet her I noticed her mitten paws and gasped. My jaw dropped in awe; I looked up at Mr. Smythe in amazement because the last time I saw paws like that was on my favorite childhood cat. The connection between us was uncanny; her therapeutic ability and her mitten paws made me wonder if it was mere coincidence or if it would somehow serve a more meaningful purpose. Our chat turned into an hour of sharing stories about the cat and learning about each other. Mr. Smythe was happy to hear that his cat was well-liked in their new neighborhood, and he encouraged me to write their joyful stories on paper for him to keep and read from time to time. Creative juices that lay dormant in me for years began flowing that day with excitement to write a tale of their journey. After gathering enough details to weave with my imagination, I was able to complete their story in time for Mr. Smythe's ninetieth birthday. He was delighted with my portrayal and uplifted by the message it delivered, so he began sharing it with others in need of a boost. Five years later it wandered into the hands of a publisher, resulting in the finished product you hold in your hands today.

Whether it was serendipity or a deeper intelligence at work, the message remains the same: *every day is a gift, every change is a lesson, every new beginning is a blessing.*

– Donna Jean Paff

"We are each gifted in a unique and important way. It is our privilege and our adventure to discover our own special light."

– Evelyn Mary Dunbar

Chapter One

A Sad Goodbye

—

Mr. Smith waved goodbye to his old Virginia home with his beloved cat, Miss Marvin, seated by his side. As the chauffeur backed the car slowly out of the driveway Mr. Smith's eyes welled with tears. Reaching for the handkerchief he always kept in his coat pocket, he felt a familiar loving nudge under his arm. It was Miss Marvin snuggling up against him, as if to say, "We still have each other." For the moment Mr. Smith felt a little better, and he responded with a loving kiss on Miss Marvin's head. He took a deep breath, let out a sigh of relief, and settled back into the soft leather seat in preparation for the long ride to Pennsylvania. Driving slowly through the small town where he had grown up, Mr. Smith gazed out the car window with a solemn look as his favorite places drifted off into the distance. The hardware store, the barber shop, his favorite café—all held people and memories that would not be forgotten. His thoughts were temporarily interrupted by an unfamiliar sound coming from the rear of the vehicle. A quick glance over his shoulder reminded him of the reason for this trip. In tow behind them was a small trailer carrying a few precious belongings to their new home up north. Miss Marvin curled up next to Mr. Smith as the car pulled onto the big highway. She began to think about the first time they had met, many years ago when she was just a kitten.

Chapter Two

A Warm Welcome

—

It was Mr. Smith who had heard Miss Marvin's faint cry for help and rescued her from a tall oak tree in his backyard after she became separated from her family during a frightful summer storm. Miss Marvin shivered as she began to recall the events of that terrible night as if it were happening at the present moment. She remembered being pushed away from her family by the strong winds, blinded by the heavy rain, and to top it off, chased by a pair of lost dogs. Her mother had warned her about dogs! Instinct told the kitten to get off the ground to avoid being attacked by the dogs, when miraculously next to her stood a tall tree with wide branches where she could escape to safety and hide until daybreak. When morning came the clouds broke apart, letting the sun shine through the giant oak leaves to dry her wet kitten fur. Miss Marvin remembered feeling dizzy and weak looking down from the loving arms of the oak tree to the ground far below. She hadn't realized how high she had climbed the night before! She began to cry out for help when, suddenly, an angel appeared in the form of Mr. Smith carrying a ladder. His hands were as gentle as his voice that day when he picked the kitten off the large branch of his favorite tree.

Miss Marvin awoke from her dream to find herself back in the car being lifted onto Mr. Smith's warm lap with that same gentleness. She stretched out her paws and yawned before drifting off to sleep again.

Chapter Three

A Trip Down Memory Lane

—

As he stroked Miss Marvin's back, Mr. Smith closed his eyes and imagined the long years of his life being played back in his mind. A smile came to his face as he pictured himself as a young man with Mrs. Smith by his side when they moved into their Virginia home together with their two young children. The family of four spent many hours playing in the big back yard or relaxing under the shade of that wonderful oak tree. He fondly recalled the day he surprised his son and daughter with a tire swing, which he tied to the strongest branch of the oak. If one sat across from the other, they could both ride at the same time! He licked his lips, almost able to taste the strawberry pie Mrs. Smith baked every Memorial Day for their annual family picnic. His head shook as he thought of the many piles of leaves they raked to jump into each fall, while the squirrels gathered the acorns that fell from the oak. He grinned as he remembered the thrill of the season's first snowfall in anticipation of enough to build a large snowman. Suddenly his memory raced ahead and his smile turned upside-down as he pictured himself at the cemetery following the burial of his dear wife of forty years. Even though Mr. Smith was half-asleep, he could consciously feel a tear stream down his cheek as he spoke out loud, "gone too soon." Wiping his tear with the hankie from his pocket, his mind returned to the fateful day when Miss Marvin came into his life at a time when they both needed a friend.

Chapter Four

What a Difference a Day Makes

—

Gazing out the window of the speeding car, Mr. Smith became entranced by the trees flashing past as they drove down the highway. He soon found himself back in time again, cleaning up the many branches and leaves scattered about his yard from the violent storm that had passed through the previous night. He recalled thinking, "what a difference a day makes," when he saw the sun peeking through the large leaves of the oak tree and heard birds singing cheerily from its branches. That tall oak stood strong through many a storm during the forty-five years he lived there. Mr. Smith remembered a faint cry coming from the tree and cupping his hands over his ears as he squinted to get a better look. He yelled, "holy moley," upon discovering a tiny kitten sitting on a branch high above the ground.

"Meow, meow," it cried in a quivering voice. And without further ado Mr. Smith hurried to get his ladder for the rescue.

Even as he presently sat in the moving car, Mr. Smith could almost feel himself carefully climbing the ladder, reaching for the frightened, shivering kitten, and gently picking it from the branch to safety. But all at once, the car swerved to miss a huge pothole in the highway. Miss Marvin was jolted off Mr. Smith's lap as he was lifted off his seat! The chauffeur apologized for the rude awakening and suggested that perhaps now would be a good time to stop for a rest and eat their lunch. Knowing it could take at least another two hours to reach their destination, Mr. Smith agreed while Miss Marvin *meowed* her approval.

Miss MARVIN
MARVIN SMITH

CHAPTER FIVE

You Fooled Me and I Fooled You

—

A few miles down the road sat a lovely picnic area just waiting for a visit from some hungry travelers. Mr. Smith directed the chauffeur to pull into a parking space close to a picnic table. Miss Marvin jumped onto the seat back for a better look. She was getting hungry herself, and needed to stretch her legs as well. Once parked, the chauffeur helped Mr. Smith out of the car with Miss Marvin close behind him.

"I'll get the cooler out of the trunk, Mr. Smith," called the chauffeur.

As they made their way to the nearby picnic table, Miss Marvin rolled around on the soft green grass to scratch her back. Then she watched patiently as they placed all the food on the table. There were two man-sized sandwiches, a bag of potato chips, a bunch of green grapes, and two bottles of water for the chauffeur and Mr. Smith. A thermos of hot coffee and two chocolate chip cookies completed their feast.

"Dig in," shouted Mr. Smith to the chauffeur. Miss Marvin cocked her head to one side with a puzzled look on her face. She couldn't believe her eyes! She was sure Mr. Smith had remembered to pack her favorite kitty treats; she was certain she had smelled them, but where were they? And Mr. Smith always gave her a bit of milk on special occasions!

As she hung her head in disappointment, Mr. Smith suddenly pulled another bag from a secret compartment and announced, "Ta da! I fooled you!" He held in his hands her favorite treats, along with milk to be served in her special travel bowl. "I may be getting old and feeble, but I'll never forget to feed my special lady friend!" Mr. Smith said as he lovingly set her place beside them at the table.

She rubbed up against his legs and purred loudly in appreciation. That old Mr. Smith still had the sense of humor Miss Marvin had grown to love during their ten years together. How lucky she always felt to have been adopted by Mr. Smith when her family could not be found. Mr. Smith, however, always felt it was he who was the lucky one, as he knew the heartsick feeling of being alone after Mrs. Smith passed away. That kitten filled his void more than she could ever imagine. This special companionship was evident to anyone who got to know Mr. Smith and Miss Marvin. Even in their short time travelling together, the chauffeur could sense they were devoted to each other.

While they enjoyed their lunch and brief rest, Mr. Smith explained to the chauffeur how this special kitty had come into his life years ago. He shared the interesting and funny details of their first visit to the veterinarian. Besides getting the necessary shots and general checkup for his new-found friend, Mr. Smith had some concerns about the unusual extra toe on each front paw and he wondered if it would be a hindrance for the kitten.

"You are looking at an American Polydactyl cat," explained the vet. "Polydactyl means multiple toes," he added. "This trait can appear in any breed. They are sometimes called mitten cats because the paw resembles a mitten. Perhaps the most famous are the ones who live at the Ernest Hemingway home in Key West, Florida, and as a result are sometimes known as a Hemingway cat." The vet went on to say that these cats seem to be more relaxed and mellow, are reported to be affectionate and patient, and some people consider the extra toe to be good luck. "I've seen a few cats with this same condition and they all seem to compensate quite well in spite of it," he explained. After the examination was completed the vet announced, "You've got a special and very healthy kitten here, Mr. Smith. However, you should consider changing one thing." Mr. Smith was puzzled. The vet grinned and winked one eye at him when he asked, "You named your kitten Marvin?"

"Yes, I did," answered Mr. Smith, still puzzled.

"Well," explained the vet, "your kitten is a female!"

"Oh, my goodness gracious," shouted a surprised Mr. Smith. After just a brief pause he decided, "Well, then I'll just add 'Miss' to the name." And Miss Marvin she was!

"Well, I'll be!" said the chauffeur as he laughed out loud. He shook his head and admitted he had been wondering about the name *Miss* Marvin all morning long.

"Mystery solved," exclaimed Mr. Smith. And they continued to chuckle while they packed up the car.

Chapter Six

Growing Up Together

—

During their years together Mr. Smith and Miss Marvin enjoyed each season to the fullest in the back yard beneath their special oak tree. They spent hot summer days lying under the umbrella of shade cast by the large leaves of the oak. Autumn brought windy days that made those leaves fall in huge piles perfect for jumping in and hiding. Short, cold days of winter were spent mostly indoors with Mr. Smith sitting in his favorite chair by the window while Miss Marvin lay on her warm braided rug, watchful for snowflakes to find rest on the oak's thick branches. They knew spring was near when birds began building nests in the protection of the old oak tree, which never seemed to show its age.

The vet had been right about that extra toe, as it never seemed to be a problem for Miss Marvin but rather distinguished her from all the other grey shorthairs with green eyes in the neighborhood. Her broad face seemed to have a permanent smile and her silky fur just begged to be touched. Some people noticed an unexplainable calmness they felt when Miss Marvin was near. Most everyone was drawn to her like a magnet.

The years seemed to pass by very quickly for these best buddies. As they grew older together physical changes started to show. Miss Marvin, no longer the playful kitten she used to be, could see Mr. Smith slowing down quite a bit, too. She instinctively knew to stay clear of his feet as he shuffled along.

To try to stay fit, Mr. Smith and the neighbor started walking around the block every morning before breakfast. One day Mr. Smith awoke with a terrible headache. He was so dizzy he had to call his neighbor to cancel their daily walk. Miss Marvin overheard Mr. Smith chuckle as he told the neighbor, "Well, I'll send Miss Marvin over if I fall down and need your help." Shortly after that call, Mr. Smith poured himself a cup of tea. As he turned around to get the honey from the shelf, a loud thud reached Miss Marvin's ears in the next room. She raced to the kitchen to find Mr. Smith on the floor.

"Help me," he moaned before passing out. Miss Marvin shot through her pet door like a bullet and ran to the next-door neighbor's porch with the speed of a much younger cat. She meowed as loudly as she could and didn't stop until the neighbor came to the door and followed her to help rescue Mr. Smith. When the ambulance arrived to take Mr. Smith to the hospital he was awake but still groggy.

"Please take care of Miss Marvin while I'm gone," he mumbled to the neighbor. Even in his weakened condition Mr. Smith did not forget about his best friend.

Chapter Seven

A Frightful Storm of Life

—

Miss Marvin sat on the windowsill all night long waiting for Mr. Smith to return home. But the sun rose and set again, and still there was no sign of him. When the neighbor came by to feed Miss Marvin, he was nice, but he wasn't Mr. Smith! When dawn arrived the next day, Miss Marvin heard a car pull into the driveway. It was Mr. Smith's daughter visiting all the way from Pennsylvania!

"Something must be terribly wrong with Mr. Smith," Miss Marvin thought.

As Mr. Smith's daughter unlocked the front door, Miss Marvin jumped off the windowsill to greet her. His daughter was as kind and gentle as Mr. Smith, and she had such a pleasant and happy smile. Miss Marvin hoped that meant her best friend was better and ready to come home to her. Very shortly after his daughter arrived, Miss Marvin saw a hospital van pull up with Mr. Smith inside. A nurse helped him get out of the van, but …

"Wait a minute," thought Miss Marvin. "What

is that big stick he is leaning on?"

Mr. Smith's daughter lovingly picked up Miss Marvin and held her gently in her arms as her father slowly made his way to the open front door. She whispered calmly as she told Miss Marvin what had happened to their loved one. She explained that he had something called a "stroke" that made him feel dizzy and fall down. The stroke made his left side weak, making it necessary for him to use a cane for balance. Worst of all, he may have to give up driving his car. Miss Marvin could sense that their lives were about to change in a big way. She seemed to be able to understand things the same way human beings do, and Miss Marvin knew the agony her best friend and constant companion would endure if he had to leave his lovely Virginia home—the home he and Mrs. Smith bought together so long ago—the home he raised his children in and the yard he enjoyed so much. He would miss that special oak tree!

As soon as Mr. Smith got settled into his favorite chair he motioned to Miss Marvin to sit on his lap. Her response was immediate and her joyful purr was so loud it could be heard in the next room where Mr. Smith's daughter and the nurse were discussing his therapy schedule. They stopped momentarily to check on the noise, which sounded like a motor running.

"Maybe these good vibrations from Miss Marvin will be therapy enough," kidded Mr. Smith. Laughter filled their home once more, and for a little while it was just like the good old days.

Mr. Smith's daughter stayed to help her father during his recovery. He loved having his "little girl" back home again, though she now had a family of her own in Pennsylvania. She really did enjoy being back in her old neighborhood, but felt torn between the needs of her loving father and those of her husband and their two growing boys. Weeks passed by with no great improvement in Mr. Smith's health and he was growing very weary. He didn't like being helpless. He missed being able to drive his car. He missed his freedom. He missed his youth! Following many discussions with his doctor, the physical therapist, and his daughter, Mr. Smith made one of the hardest decisions he had ever made in his entire life: to move to Pennsylvania. Miss Marvin felt his pain along with him, but would do whatever it took to keep him safe.

Chapter Eight

New Beginnings

—

As the chauffeur pulled the car into the parking lot of the New Beginnings Retirement Home in Pennsylvania, he called to Mr. Smith and Miss Marvin, “We have arrived, Sir and Madam!”

They both yawned and stretched out their arms as they looked out the car windows to see their new home. Mr. Smith’s stomach suddenly felt a bit unsettled, and for a moment he thought he might get sick. Sensing his agony, Miss Marvin nudged his arm, as if to say, “It will be all right.” The chauffeur helped Mr. Smith get out of the car with Miss Marvin tucked under his arm. Mr. Smith saw his daughter, her husband, and their two boys cheerfully waiting to greet them with a bouquet of balloons. The boys hadn’t seen their grandfather in person since the Easter before his stroke. It shocked them to see this once-energetic, spry man now pale and thin and too weak to walk without a cane. This was not the man they remembered, and it scared them a little. Suddenly Miss Marvin jumped down from Mr. Smith's arms. She, too, was scared. She was not fond of balloons!

"Boys, you surely remember Miss Marvin," said Mr. Smith. "How would you like to show her our new place?" He asked encouragingly. At that moment, a nurse appeared at the door pushing a large cart to carry Mr. Smith's suitcases and smaller packages. She helped him with his bags as her assistant began to load onto a dolly the few pieces of furniture Mr. Smith was allowed to bring with him. Once the luggage was secure, they all followed the nurse to ride the elevator to the third floor apartment waiting for them. Miss Marvin had never ridden in an elevator before, and she tried to be brave in the arms of Mr. Smith's older grandson as she experienced the upward motion but was unable to see where she was going. When the elevator came to a stop, a bell rang and the door opened up to a long hallway leading to their new home.

With the help of his family, Mr. Smith tried to make the small apartment look and feel like his old Virginia home. He placed his favorite chair beside the window and laid Miss Marvin's braided rug nearby. A few familiar pictures were hung on the walls and some of his favorite books were arranged on the shelf by his bed. The television now sat on his dresser top, as the living room was also the bedroom. A kitchenette with a short countertop held a tiny microwave for Mr. Smith to make his hot tea or coffee. Beneath the counter stood a couple of bar stools and a small refrigerator to hold cold drinks or snacks for Mr. Smith, along with cat food and "special occasion" milk for Miss Marvin. There was no need for a dining table in their apartment since all meals would be made by the New Beginnings chef and served in the main dining hall for all residents of this retirement community. A brand new kitty-litter box with a privacy lid for Miss Marvin sat inside the compact bathroom. These were the only belongings, with the exception of Mr. Smith's clothing, that he was allowed to bring. Of all the things they had to leave behind, the backyard with the old oak tree was missed the most!

New
Beginnings

Chapter Nine

Miss Marvin's First Visit

—

Throughout the next few weeks, Mr. Smith and Miss Marvin became familiar with their new surroundings and got acquainted with a few of their many neighbors. Miss Marvin rested in Mr. Smith's arms while she was introduced to sights, sounds, and smells she never knew existed. While some residents sat on chairs with wheels pushed by nurses, others pushed carts on wheels while walking behind at a turtle's pace. Some used canes like Mr. Smith. A few walked without assistance but shuffled their feet, much like Mr. Smith did before his fall. Miss Marvin knew to stay clear to avoid being stepped on or, worst of all, cause someone to trip over her and fall down.

Their daily lives changed drastically over the course of a few weeks. In contrast to the carefree life they lived in Virginia, they now had a scheduled, almost rigid existence. Mr. Smith left the apartment for breakfast, lunch, and dinner every day. Oh, how Miss Marvin missed the smell of his home cooking! Even more than that, however, she missed his company as now he spent much of the day visiting and talking with his new friends. Once or twice each week his daughter would come by and take Mr. Smith away for the entire day, leaving Miss Marvin all alone in that small apartment with no back yard. Time dragged on as she waited for Mr. Smith to return and pay her some undivided attention. In her feline heart, she was glad her master had grown content with his new life, but now she longed for that same contentment.

One day Mr. Smith overslept, and as he hurried out the door to get to breakfast he accidentally left the door to their apartment ajar. Now was her chance to step outside the walls of the apartment on her own. She slowly peeked around the door and saw the coast was clear. The next-door neighbor would be a good place to start, she thought, so she tiptoed over and sat by the door. This was the home of Mr. and Mrs. Miller, who were always soft spoken and kind to everyone. Perhaps they would like a visit from Miss Marvin. So she began to meow softly in a very ladylike manner. A few moments later, the door opened to reveal the Millers with the sweetest smiles on their faces.

"Well look here," exclaimed a surprised Mr. Miller. "We have a special visitor, Mrs. Miller."

His wife joined in and they both asked in unison, "Won't you please come in, Miss Marvin?"

Miss Marvin cautiously walked into the Millers' apartment and looked around. It seemed very much the same as the apartment she and Mr. Smith shared, except for the furnishings. Mr. Miller showed Miss Marvin his favorite easy chair, which was seated beside a large window. He encouraged her to jump up for a look outside. They even politely asked first before petting her. Miss Marvin wanted to stay longer, but knew she had better get back before Mr. Smith found her gone. He would surely be worried. So she jumped down from the easy chair and walked to the door.

"Thank you for your visit, Miss Marvin," her hosts said sincerely.

"And please feel free to visit us any time," added Mr. Miller as he opened the door to let her out. She scampered back through the still-ajar apartment door, feeling proud that she had found the courage to explore her new world.

"Tomorrow," she thought, "I'll walk down the hallway to meet someone else!"

That evening at dinner, the Millers told Mr. Smith the funny story of how his haste in not closing his apartment door had led to a delightful surprise visit from Miss Marvin that morning. They even expressed hope she could visit again. Mr. Smith was glad to hear his neighbors speak so joyfully about his pet, and he was willing to share this love with others.

Chapter Ten

Miss Marvin Explores

—

As soon as Mr. Smith opened his door the next morning to retrieve his newspaper, Miss Marvin squeezed through the door and looked back at her companion for his approval before leaving.

"Go ahead, kitty," Mr. Smith said kindly. "There are some nice folks just waiting for a visit from Miss Marvin." He seemed to know exactly what she was thinking.

As Miss Marvin padded her way down the long hall, a nurse stepped outside one of the apartments. Upon spotting the cat she called out to the resident inside.

"Mary, are you expecting a visitor?" Asked the nurse. "There's a beautiful cat waiting to see you." She pushed the apartment door open and stepped to one side.

Miss Marvin peeked inside and saw a lady seated on one of those chairs with wheels. She was wearing a tube under her nose which led to a large noisy machine sitting beside her chair. Miss

Marvin instinctively responded to this sight and sound by arching her back in fear.

As the cat began to back away, Mary called to her in a kind and gentle voice. “Don’t be afraid, kitty-cat. This machine helps me breathe,” she explained calmly.

After a little coaxing from Mary, Miss Marvin cautiously entered the room and looked around. The brightly-colored afghan on Mary’s lap caught her attention because it looked just like one Mr. Smith had used back in their old Virginia home.

“Would you like to sit on my lap, kitty?” asked Mary. “It’s nice and warm,” she added persuasively.

Miss Marvin found the invitation hard to resist and hopped up. Almost instantly she felt comfortable and soon forgot about the scary machine and its noise. She began purring and kneading Mary’s afghan with her front paws.

“Oh, you have special Hemingway cat paws,” Mary stated matter-of-factly.

Miss Marvin stopped purring for a moment and gazed up at Mary in amazement, wondering how this ancient, sickly woman knew that. Perhaps Mr. Smith was right when he often said “Don’t judge a book by its cover.”

Mary slowly stroked Miss Marvin's soft fur, which brought to mind the feel of the mink stole her husband had bought her on their tenth wedding anniversary. This thought prompted Mary to share some of her warm memories with her new acquaintance. Her gentle touch and soothing voice put Miss Marvin in a state of relaxation that she hadn't felt in a very long time. She began to purr loudly while Mary continued her story, explaining how years of smoking cigarettes had left her lungs weak, now making it necessary to use a machine to assist her in breathing. She described how the tubes carried the oxygen to her nasal passages, and how the chair with wheels allowed her to travel almost anywhere she needed to go in the building, since she no longer had the strength to walk on her own. Miss Marvin felt at ease with this knowledge, and had nearly drifted off to sleep when a knock came at the door.

"It's time for lunch, Mary," said a cheery voice on the other side of the door.

With Miss Marvin still seated on her lap, Mary wheeled herself over to the door and opened it to find the next-door neighbor lady standing there.

"Oh, you have a visitor," the surprised neighbor

announced when she spied the cat on Mary's lap.

"Yes, I do, Ruth. I'd love to introduce you to one of the best listeners in this place," bragged Mary, "but I do not know her name."

At that moment an aide arrived to help Mary switch her oxygen from the big machine to a portable tank that hung on the back of her wheelchair for whenever she needed to leave her room.

"Can you solve this mystery for us, young man?" asked Mary.

"I most certainly can," stated the aide. "This cat is Mr. Smith's companion and her name is Miss Marvin," he explained.

Miss Marvin sensed it was time for her to leave her new friend for now. She jumped off Mary's warm lap and started walking slowly toward Mr. Smith's apartment. She glanced back briefly to see Mary look up at Ruth with a twinkle in her eye, and then she heard a faint whisper.

"Perhaps you'd like a visit from Miss Marvin, Ruth?"

Ruth's eyes lit up. "Oh, you know, I have a wide windowsill that gets the afternoon sun. I'll bet Miss Marvin would love to take a nap there," she exclaimed.

Chapter Eleven
The Sunny Side of Life

—

While Mary and Ruth sat in the dining room enjoying soup and tea sandwiches, Miss Marvin scampered back to her apartment to finish the few morsels of cat food she had left in her dish from breakfast that morning. Afterward, as she began to wash her whiskers, she noticed the entry lamp was lit, indicating that Mr. Smith would be gone until dark today. That meant she could feel free to pay a visit to Ruth all afternoon. She was eager to feast her eyes on that wide windowsill—something Mr. Smith's apartment did not have. Miss Marvin licked herself clean and then left the apartment again to wait patiently at Ruth's door. She listened for the sound of the elevator bell which meant Ruth was back from lunch. She wanted to surprise Ruth with her visit! As Ruth turned the corner from the elevator she could see Miss Marvin waiting at her door, and she was delighted!

"Oh my stars!" rejoiced Ruth from down the hall as she clapped her hands together in joy. "What did I do to deserve a visit from Miss Marvin?" Ruth didn't use a cane, nor did she push a cart, but she held on tightly to the railing along the wall as she inched her way to her door. "Now let me find my key and unlock my door, kitty," she said breathlessly. As she turned the knob and opened the door, the scent of roses filled the air. "Please come in and take a look around my place," Ruth commanded. "I have a beautiful view from my front window, and it gets sunshine all afternoon," she declared. "Why, I should say, it's the next best thing to actually being outside!"

Miss Marvin carefully stepped past Ruth and entered her apartment. The smell of roses grew stronger as she got closer to the window. Miss Marvin stopped dead in her tracks and blinked her cat eyes in disbelief. The wonderful wide windowsill was covered entirely with vases of roses! There was no space left on the sill for her to bask in the warm afternoon sunlight as Ruth had promised. Disappointed, she hissed and backed away from the roses, and Ruth then remembered.

"Oh my stars—the roses!" she yelled at the top of her lungs, holding her head in amazement. "You see, it was my birthday last week and my four children all sent me my favorite flower," she explained. "But I can't smell any more so I forget all about them. Isn't that something, kitten? Here now, you just wait a bit and I'll get help to move them so you can jump up and bask in the sunlight all afternoon if you want," Ruth comforted. As she picked up her phone to dial for help, a nurse's aide appeared in the doorway, still open from all the excitement.

"What's all the commotion in here, Ruth?" questioned the aide.

Ruth explained the situation and a few minutes later Miss Marvin was basking in the warm sunlight, just like Ruth had promised!

It didn't take long for Miss Marvin to fall asleep on Ruth's wide windowsill. Likewise, Ruth snored the afternoon away in her comfy recliner. As the sun dropped lower in the sky, so did the warmth, and Miss Marvin awoke feeling better than she had in quite some time. She jumped down from the windowsill with a thud which woke Ruth from her nap.

"Oh, I guess you need to go home now, kitty," Ruth said in a groggy voice. "But I do hope you'll come back to visit me soon," she added sincerely. "We have so much more to learn about each other."

With that, Ruth groaned and worked her way

out of her recliner to see Miss Marvin to the door. Standing by the open door, Ruth felt Miss Marvin brush up against her legs as she passed by, in appreciation for a delightful afternoon.

"You are very welcome, kitty, for I enjoy your company as much as you enjoy my windowsill," Ruth whispered happily.

When she arrived at the apartment door, Miss Marvin was able to slip through the opening that Mr. Smith left slightly ajar for her to come and go as she pleased. She found some of her favorite cat food waiting in her familiar plastic bowl with fresh water alongside. Even when he was not there, somehow Mr. Smith made certain that Miss Marvin wasn't forgotten. As day turned into night, Miss Marvin waited patiently for Mr. Smith to come home to show him how much better she felt about the changes in their lives. Just as her internal clock told her it was time, she heard the elevator bell ring and, sure enough, seconds later Mr. Smith walked through the apartment door. The two old friends greeted each other more joyfully than in recent memory.

"To everything there is a season, and a time for every purpose under the heaven!"

Chapter Twelve
Glory Hallelujah

—

Summer turned to autumn at the retirement home in Pennsylvania, and by now Miss Marvin and Mr. Smith were used to their daily routine. Miss Marvin kept herself busy several times a week with her visits to the Millers, Mary, and Ruth. Sunday mornings were the quietest, when most people slept in longer or read their Sunday newspaper until it was time for Sunday brunch in the New Beginnings dining room. Some people went to the church service held in the chapel, which just happened to be across the hall from Mr. Smith's third-floor apartment. Every Sunday since they had moved in four months ago, Miss Marvin heard the congregation singing praises to God and saying "Glory hallelujah." She watched Mary painfully wheel herself inside the chapel each week and then exit with a huge uplifted smile on her face after the service.

Mr. Smith loved God, too. He had shared stories of lambs and lions and a special donkey with Miss

Marvin back in their Virginia home. He always thanked God for his food before he ate and said a prayer for others before he went to sleep at night. Shortly after moving to Pennsylvania, Mr. Smith joined his daughter and her family for worship at their church in a community near the New Beginnings Retirement Home. Now Miss Marvin longed to experience a church service and to sit inside a real chapel.

When the next Sunday morning arrived, Miss Marvin ate her breakfast early, licked herself clean, and quietly made her way across the hall to the chapel door. People were already arriving and the candles were lit at the altar. As usual, Mary was slowly making her way down the hall in her wheelchair. As she approached the door she was taken by surprise to see Miss Marvin sitting there.

Mary's pained expression changed to an astonished smile as she gasped excitedly, "Well, look who is coming to church, everyone." She politely added, "After you, Miss Marvin," as she directed the cat to an empty seat alongside her.

Miss Marvin was stunned that she would be invited to jump up and actually sit on a seat intended for one of the people. She felt very much honored, indeed, and very uplifted already! The positive energy that flowed within that small chapel made everyone glow, and Miss Marvin felt a renewed life emerging from her old feline body. She now understood the feeling of being blessed. This detour that she and Mr. Smith needed to take in life had been a blessing in the form of knowledge. She now knew her purpose, and she was ready to give others a visit from Miss Marvin!

A Miss Marvin "Short"

—

This poetic version of *A Visit From Miss Marvin* was written as a quick and easy way to understand the message the story relays. Readers who are too busy for twelve chapters or who have limited sight or reading skills will find this poem delightful in its own right. It can also be used as an overview prior to reading the book, or simply as an inspirational piece.

Once upon a time in Virginia...

Mr. Smith rescued a kitten from his favorite
  backyard tree.
He tried and tried but could not find the
  kitten's family.
So Mr. Smith politely asked if the kitten would
  like to stay.
For he was all alone, as well, and looking for a
  friend to play.

"You need a name," said Mr. Smith, so he
named the kitty Marvin.
And then he set a bowl of food to keep the cat
from starvin'.

"Next thing we need is for the vet to meet my
new companion."
But on that day the vet announced, "There's
something that needs changin'.
Your kitty is quite healthy, though might not
like to be
Called by a name like Marvin—for your kitty
is a she!"

"Oh goodness gracious!" gasped Mr. Smith.
"Then I'll simply have to add a Miss!"
They laughed and laughed and went away
With closer feelings for each other that day.

These two new friends spent time together
Inside and outside in all kinds of weather.
Their favorite tree never seemed to grow old,
But as years flew by a new story would unfold.

Once upon a time in Pennsylvania…

In elder years these two best buds
Found a new place to lay their duds.
A new beginning near his daughter
and grands
Made the process of aging a bit easier to stand.

It was during this time that they found
a new purpose.
There was actually more to life than just
playing the circus.
Mr. Smith and Miss Marvin made lots
of new friends,
Which helped them to feel like this wasn't
the end.

While her companion was out Miss Marvin
took heed
And visited the people in desperate need
Of someone to listen, someone to be there
On the lap of an elder confined to a chair.

A new life emerged from the kindness
    they shared
As the people who lived there found someone
    who cared.
They soon had forgotten their worries
    and woes
And replaced them with laughter, with bangles
    and bows.

Mr. Smith and Miss Marvin will never forget
That tree in their past, but they have
    no regrets—
For their future is bright, and they know
    it will last
Forever and ever!

About the Author

—

Where does a sixty-six-year-old begin to describe herself in a brief summary? Which talent or achievement does she list?

After contemplating my life and its many directions, I believe it is my gift of imagination that most brings me joy. From creating childhood plays with my sisters to perform for our parents and their friends, to designing haunted Halloween trails in adulthood, to present-day concocting of plots for detective parties for my grandchildren, I've had so much fun and enjoyment along the way. Interestingly, I choose nonfiction as my favorite reading material. In addition, I have a great appreciation of natural remedies, local history, and family genealogy. I'm not all fantasy. Above all, family and friends are most important to me as I spend my retirement enjoying the simple life.

– *Donna Jean Paff*

About the Illustrator

—

Simplicity and an innate love of Nature exemplify my Soul, and Life thus far has granted me many broad experiences for which I am ever grateful. Such occasions have enabled me to practice holistic healing while dabbling in small personal creative outlets such as poetry, floral design, and sculpture. Alternately, my career as a Dental Hygienist has allowed me to fulfill my passion for helping others while simultaneously affording me the satisfaction of working with my hands. The opportunity to collaborate with my mother on *A Visit From Miss Marvin* has been both invigorating and humbling. My heart swells with joy and appreciation.

– *Bella Viva*

CPSIA information can be obtained
at www.ICGtesting.com
Printed in the USA
BVHW030015190619
551380BV00001B/19/P